Chicago

Chicago

A Downtown America Book

Christine Pfeiffer

dP Dillon Press, Inc. Minneapolis, MN 55415

Photographic Acknowledgments

The photographs are reproduced through the courtesy of the Chicago Historical Society; Chicago Tourism Council; Terry Farmer, Illinois Department of Commerce and Community Affairs; Jane Addams Memorial Collection, Special Collections, the University Library, University of Illinois at Chicago; Lincoln Park Zoological Society; Milt and Joan Mann, Cameramann International; Museum of Science and Industry, Chicago; Nghia Sinh International; Christine Pfeiffer; Serbian Cultural Club. Title page: sailboats on Lake Michigan, Chuck L'Heureux. Cover: Chicago downtown skyline, Gary Milburn/Tom Stack & Associates.

Library of Congress Cataloging-in-Publication Data

Pfeiffer, Christine.
Chicago / by Christine Pfeiffer.
(A Downtown America book)
Includes index.
Summary: Introduces the city of Chicago, both past and present, describing neighborhoods, attractions, and festivals.
1. Chicago (Ill.)—Juvenile literature. [1. Chicago (Ill.)]
I. Title. II. Series.
F548.33.P44 1988   977.3'11   88-20199
ISBN 0-87518-385-9

Dillon Press, Inc., 242 Portland Avenue South
Minneapolis, Minnesota 55415

Printed in the United States of America
 2 3 4 5 6 7 8 9 10 97 96 95 94 93 92 91 90

About the Author

Chicagoan Christine Pfeiffer brings nearly twenty years of experience to writing about the Windy City. She teaches English composition and writing at Oakton College in the Chicago area. An experienced educational writer, Ms. Pfeiffer has written for several cultural organizations and many educational magazines. She is the author of *Germany: Two Nations, One Heritage* and *Poland: Land of Freedom Fighters*, both Dillon Press Discovering Our Heritage books. Her educational background includes a master's degree from Northwestern University.

Contents

Fast Facts about Chicago

Chicago: The Windy City, The Second City, The City That Works, City of Parks City of the Big Shoulders

Location: Northeast corner of Illinois, along 29 miles (46.7 kilometers) of the southwest coast of Lake Michigan

Area: City, 228 square miles (591 square kilometers); consolidated metropolitan area, 5,694 square miles (14,747 square kilometers)

Population (1986 estimate*): City, 3,009,530; consolidated metropolitan area, 8,116,100

Major Population Groups: Blacks, Mexicans, Poles, Germans, Irish, Italians, Puerto Ricans, Russians, Greeks, Filipinos, Swedes, Chinese, Ukrainians, Asian Indians

Altitude: 578.5 feet (176 meters)

Climate: Average temperature is 25°F (-4° C) in January, 75°F (24°C) in July; average annual precipitation, including rain and snow, is 33 inches (84 centimeters)

Founding Date: Incorporated as a city on March 4, 1837

City Flag: White with two horizontal blue stripes, symbolizing the two branches of the Chicago River, above and below four red stars, symbolizing Fort Dearborn, the Great Fire, and the Chicago expositions

City Seal: Round blue border with gold letters "City of Chicago, incorporated 4th March 1837;" motto on red band *Urbs in Horto* ("City in a Garden"); center scene has sailing ship on Lake Michigan, Indian standing on shore, child in seashell (symbolizing peace and purity), shield (national spirit) with sheaf of wheat (harvest plenty)

Form of Government: Mayor-council; city council is made up of aldermen representing each of the city's fifty wards; mayor must get approval from city council on important decisions; mayor and council members are elected for four years.

Important Industries: Construction, printing and publishing, food production, industrial and medical research, wholesale and retail trade, banking, trading of stocks and agricultural commodities, advertising

*U.S. Bureau of the Census 1988 population estimates available in fall 1989; official 1990 census figures available in 1991-92.

Festivals and Parades

February: Black History Month events; Chinese New Year celebration (Chinatown)

March: St. Patrick's Day Parade, ceremony dying the Chicago River green; St. Joseph's Day (Italian community)

April: Easter basket blessing (Polish and Ukrainian churches); Arbor Day tree planting (Grant Park)

May: International Art Expo; Polish Constitution Day Parade; Memorial Day Parade

June: Chicago Blues Festival; Old Town Art Fair

July: Air and Water Show; Taste of Chicago; Fourth of July concert and fireworks (Grant Park) and show (Soldier Field)

August: Gold Coast Art Fair; Ginza Festival (Japanese Buddhist Temple); Venetian Night

September: Mexican Independence Day Parade; Von Steuben Day Parade; Chicago Jazz Festival; Taste of Polonia

October: American Indian History Month events; Chinese Independence Day procession (Chinatown); Columbus Day Parade

November: Veterans' Day Parade; Chicago International Film Festival; Santa Claus Parade

December: Giant Christmas tree decoration ceremony (Daley Plaza); "Christmas Around the World" exhibit (Museum of Science and Industry); Caroling to the Animals (Lincoln Park Zoo)

For further information about festivals and parades, see agencies listed on page 57.

United States

CANADA

WASHINGTON
★ Seattle
★ Olympia
Portland •

OREGON
★ Salem

MONTANA
★ Helena

IDAHO
• Boise

NORTH DAKOTA
★ Bismarck

MINNESOTA
Minneapolis •
St. Paul ★

SOUTH DAKOTA
★ Pierre

WYOMING
★ Cheyenne

Great Salt Lake

NEVADA
★ Carson City

Sacramento ★
San Francisco •

CALIFORNIA
• Los Angeles
• San Diego

Las Vegas •

UTAH
Salt Lake City ★

ARIZONA
★ Phoenix
• Tucson

Albuquerque •

NEW MEXICO

★ Santa Fe

COLORADO
Denver ★

NEBRASKA
Lincoln ★ • Omaha

IOWA
Des Moines ★

KANSAS
Topeka ★ • Kansas City
Jefferson City ★

MISSOURI
St. Louis •

WISCONSIN
Madison ★
Milwaukee •

Lake Superior

Lake Michigan

Lake Huron

MICHIGAN
Lansing ★
Detroit •

Lake Ontario

Lake Erie

MINNESOTA

Mississippi

CHICAGO

ILLINOIS
Springfield ★

INDIANA
Indianapolis ★

OHIO
Columbus ★
Cincinnati •
Cleveland •

Louisville •

KENTUCKY
Frankfort ★

TENNESSEE
★ Nashville
Memphis •

OKLAHOMA
Oklahoma City ★
Tulsa •

ARKANSAS
Little Rock ★

NEW HAMPSHIRE
VERMONT
Montpelier ★

MAINE
★ Augusta

Concord ★

MASSACHUSETTS
Albany ★ Boston ★
• Providence

Hartford ★

RHODE ISLAND

CONNECTICUT

NEW YORK
Trenton ★ New York City

NEW JERSEY

PENNSYLVANIA
Pittsburgh • Harrisburg ★
Philadelphia •

Baltimore •

DELAWARE
Dover ★

Annapolis ★

Washington, D.C. ⊕

MARYLAND

WEST VIRGINIA
Charleston ★

Richmond ★

VIRGINIA

NORTH CAROLINA
★ Raleigh
Charlotte •

SOUTH CAROLINA
Columbia ★

GEORGIA
★ Montgomery
★ Atlanta

ALABAMA
Birmingham •
Montgomery ★

MISSISSIPPI
Jackson ★

LOUISIANA
Baton Rouge ★ • New Orleans

TEXAS
Fort Worth • • Dallas
San Antonio • Austin ★
Houston •

El Paso •

Rio Grande

MEXICO

Pacific Ocean

Atlantic Ocean

FLORIDA
Tallahassee ★
St. Petersburg • Tampa •
Jacksonville •
• Miami

Gulf of Mexico

U.S.S.R.

ALASKA
• Anchorage
Juneau ★

CANADA

Honolulu •

HAWAII

Chicago

Points of Interest

- A Chicago Public Library Cultural Center
- B Field Museum of Natural History, John G. Shedd Aquarium, Adler Planetarium
- C Museum of Science and Industry
- D Art Institute of Chicago
- E Lincoln Park Zoo
- F Wrigley Field
- G Soldier Field
- H Comiskey Park
- I Sears Tower
- J John Hancock Center
- K O'Hare International Airport
- L Midway Airport

N

Lake Michigan

Chicago River

NORTH SIDE

NEW TOWN

OLD TOWN

LINCOLN PARK

GOLD COAST

WEST SIDE

GRANT PARK

Sanitary and Ship Canal

BURNHAM PARK

Lake Shore Drive

SOUTH SIDE

JACKSON PARK

ILLINOIS

INDIANA

| 0 | 5 | 10 | miles |
| 0 | 5 | 10 | 15 | kilometers |

1

Chicago, Chicago

Imagine a city that has some of the world's tallest and most beautiful buildings along a lake that looks as big as the ocean. Every kind of person you can imagine—of all ages and all colors, speaking many different languages, from nearly every country in the world—lives in the city. In its stores you find all kinds of wonderful clothes, toys, art, games, televisions, and just about everything else a person could want to buy. In its many parks, some along the lake, you discover playgrounds and swimming pools, softball diamonds, and people acting in plays. Without going far from home, you see an incredible variety of ocean life, watch what the stars looked like a hundred years ago, and touch a dinosaur skeleton.

People who live in Chicago don't have to imagine these things. They al-

The skyscrapers of downtown Chicago rise along the shores of Lake Michigan.

Alexander Calder's *Flamingo* brightens a plaza in downtown Chicago.

ready live in a city that has them all!

Chicago is one of the world's greatest cities. It is great not only in size—the third-largest U.S. city after New York and Los Angeles—but in importance. Almost everything that could possibly be in a city is some-where in Chicago. It is a center for industry, banking, publishing, enter-tainment, transportation, and for buy-ing and selling many different prod-ucts and services. It has one of the world's busiest airports, the largest grain market, and the tallest buildings.

On a hot summer's day, Chicagoans relax by the lake at Lincoln Park.

This huge city lies at the northern end of Illinois, along Lake Michigan, one of the Great Lakes. Chicago has four main parts—the downtown area, and the West, North, and South sides. Because it borders Lake Michigan, the city has no "East Side."

Parks cover much of Chicago's beautiful lakefront area. Jackson and Burnham parks on the South Side, Grant Park near downtown, and Lincoln Park on the North Side stretch for miles along Lake Michigan. Lincoln Park, Chicago's largest and most popular park, has sandy beaches, lagoons, and a zoo. In the summer, thousands of Chicagoans enjoy their parks on the lake each day.

Lake Michigan is very important to Chicago. Through the Great Lakes, huge ships can bring fuel, supplies, and all kinds of products into the city. Most of the water that Chicagoans drink and bathe in comes from the lake. The lake has a big effect on Chicago's weather, too. Fog, "lake effect" snow, and storms that sometimes splash people's cars or flood their apartments can often be blamed on Lake Michigan. During the summer the lake helps cool the city, and especially cools those people who go to the beach and jump into the cold water.

Even when it's not swimming weather, people like to walk by the lake, drive or bicycle along it, go sailing on it, or look at it from skyscraper windows. In winter, its edge freezes into huge ice chunks. At other times it changes color from blue to green, aqua to gray, and may be rough and stormy or smooth as glass. Chicago wouldn't seem like Chicago without its lake.

Wind is another natural feature that makes Chicagoans feel right at home. In fact, "The Windy City" is one of Chicago's nicknames. In winter, there are often strong, cold winds that can make it difficult to open doors or hang onto a hat. But the real reason for this name goes back to the 1893 World's Fair. Chicago officials

bragged so much about the Columbian Exposition that a New York editor made a remark about all the "hot air" coming from the Windy City.

Like other places in the Midwest, Chicago has four seasons. Most Chicagoans would describe them this way: a very beautiful few days of spring; a long, hot summer that arrives before people have put their winter coats away; a wonderful crisp fall that usually lasts several weeks; and a very long, very cold winter with too much snow and too much wind.

Since Chicago is such a good place to find almost every kind of work, people come to the city whether or not they like the climate. Large and small companies, offices that provide many kinds of services, stores

Lincoln Park lies along Lake Michigan on Chicago's North Side. Starting near the downtown area, the park stretches for miles along the lake.

of all kinds, restaurants, some of the world's biggest banks—Chicago has them all. It has thousands of doctors, lawyers, artists, writers, and actors. Such a big city also needs many police officers, fire fighters, teachers, mail carriers, and other kinds of city and county government workers. At the Chicago Post Office, the world's largest post office building, 14,700 workers handle about 4 billion pieces of mail each year.

Though Chicago is not the Illinois state capital, the Chicago city government is much larger than the governments of some states. Since Chicago is in Cook County, it is a center of county government, too.

Skyscrapers are one feature of Chicago that show it is a very large

The Sears Tower at night.

and busy city. A building that is 30 or 50 stories high is ordinary in Chicago. Driving along Lake Shore Drive, between Lake Michigan and the city skyline, Chicagoans and visitors can see an incredible variety of tall buildings. The snowy-white Wrigley Building (the home of chewing gum) is always lit at night. Chicago's largest newspaper has its offices in the grand Tribune Tower. Lake Point Tower is a sleek apartment building based on a design by Mies Van Der Rohe, a famous German architect.

Some big companies such as Sears, John Hancock Insurance, and Amoco Oil have their own extra-tall skyscrapers. The Sears Tower, the world's tallest building, is 110 stories high, and the others are only a few stories shorter. Imagine eating lunch at The Ninety-Fifth on the 95th floor of the Hancock building, or going to the observation floor of any of these giant skyscrapers to see the city.

Part of Chicago's downtown is called the Loop, because the El (elevated train) makes a loop right in the heart of the city. Big buildings, important businesses, well-known stores and shops, and other attractions are in the Loop. But there are many other interesting places, too. Chicago is a city in which you can find almost anything, if you know where to look.

2

City of the Big Shoulders

Long ago, the Chicago area was swampland and a prairie near the settlements of several groups of native Americans. The name *Chicago* probably comes from a Potawatomi Indian word, *Che-ca-gou*, which means "wild onions" or "skunk cabbage."

Several French explorers passed through the area and marked it on their maps. But the first non-Indian settler didn't arrive until 1779. He was Jean Baptiste Pointe du Sable, a French-speaking black fur trader from New Orleans. He, his Indian wife, and their three children established the first trading post in the future city.

In 1803, a group of American soldiers came to the small settlement and built Fort Dearborn. After the American Revolution, the new United States wanted to expand westward.

Visitors to the Du Sable Museum admire a quilt that shows Jean Baptiste Pointe du Sable in front of his trading post by the lake.

Since the native Americans wanted to keep their land, some fought against the white soldiers and settlers who came to the Chicago area. In 1812, Fort Dearborn was burned, and many people were killed in one of these battles. By 1837, when Chicago became a city, only a small number of native Americans remained.

Chicago now had its first school, hotel, newspapers, theater, meat packers, and other businesses. When canals, roads, and railroads were built, Chicago grew even faster as a trade and shipping center for midwestern agricultural products.

Streets in the Chicago of the 1850s were a muddy, sloppy mess. People made jokes about horses and wagons disappearing because they sank into the mud. Street level was only a few feet above the lake, and the muddy streets and overflowing sewers caused health problems.

Then Chicago leaders came up with a crazy idea: Let's raise the whole city! This tremendous construction project raised streets and sidewalks nearly ten feet (three meters) with landfill and construction. As a result, the old "ground floors" were underground. Some buildings were remodeled, but many were actually lifted up in the air while new foundations were added. An entire hotel, the Tremont, was lifted eight feet by 500 men and 2,500 jacks. All the hotel's furniture and guests stayed inside, and not even a glass was broken!

The uplifted Chicago continued

The center of Chicago after the Great Fire of 1871.

to grow even more rapidly, and by 1870 there were nearly 300,000 Chicagoans. As the city became more crowded, fire became a big danger.

Late on October 8, 1871, after a hot, very dry summer, a fire started in the O'Learys' barn on DeKoven Street. According to legend, Mrs. O'Leary's cow kicked over a lantern left in the barn, but no one really knows for sure. This was no ordinary fire. Great mansions and rickety tenements, hotels, businesses, city buildings—all were completely destroyed.

People ran into the streets, saving what little they could, and kept moving ahead of the raging flames. Some waded out into Lake Michigan for protection. When the fire finally died, 300 people were dead, and nearly 100,000 were homeless. Within 27 hours, the entire center of the city burned to the ground.

Chicago started to rebuild immediately. Cities all over the world sent money, supplies, and enough books to give Chicago the largest public library of its time. Busy architects designed new stores, government buildings, mansions, hotels, and whole blocks of houses. The city passed new construction laws, too, so that buildings would be less likely to burn.

Soon Chicago was booming again.

Railroads and shipping had hardly been damaged by the fire. Old businesses were rebuilt, and new ones begun. Two giant meat packing firms, Armour and Swift, soon made Chicago the meat packing capital of the world. Department stores (Marshall Field's; Carson, Pirie, Scott) and mail order houses (Sears, Roebuck; Montgomery Ward's) made the city a shopping capital, too. Manufacturing grew, especially when new steel-making processes were developed.

Growing industry needed more workers. Starting in the 1800s, many Europeans came to Chicago—Germans, Poles, Irish, Italians, Swedes, Bohemians, Greeks, and others. By 1890, two of every three Chicagoans had been born in Europe. Many were poor and worked 12 or even 18 hours a day in industry.

Crowded, unsafe housing, illness, and hunger often made life difficult for these immigrants. In an attempt to help them, Jane Addams started Hull House in 1889. At Hull House people could get food and clothing, take English lessons and other classes, and talk to social workers who cared about their problems.

Although life in Chicago could be hard in the late 1800s, it was also a time of exciting growth for the city. Museums, parks, grand hotels, theaters, an orchestra, and other attractions made Chicago a city of wealth and culture as well as hard work.

Chicago celebrated when it hosted the Columbian Exposition, the

Jane Addams provided help for thousands of immigrants at Hull House.

World's Fair of 1893, in Jackson Park. Exhibits at the fair represented many countries, every U.S. state, and special fields such as agriculture, transportation, women's achievements, machinery, and fine arts. A huge Ferris wheel gave visitors an exciting view, and gondolas (like those of Venice, Italy) took people through the park along canals. The world-famous Museum of Science and Industry was built for this huge fair.

Chicago's rapid growth caused problems as well. Sewage from the city passed into the Chicago River, which flowed into Lake Michigan. As more and more people lived in the city, large amounts of sewage polluted the lake. Finally, in 1900, engineers reversed the flow of the river to

Today the Chicago River runs by the Wrigley Building in downtown Chicago.

prevent the city's sewage from flowing into the lake. When the project was completed, the Chicago River became the first river ever to flow away from its mouth.

Chicago's industry, and immigration to the city, continued to grow until World War I. The First World War brought many economic and political changes to the city. Europeans were under pressure to become "more American" because of wartime fears of spies. Suburbs grew northward along the lake shore, and some towns were made part of the city. Thousands of blacks arrived from the South to work in war industries. Chicago had become a huge city of 3 million people.

After the war, Prohibition affect-

ed Chicagoans in other ways. From 1920 to 1933, it was against the law to sell beer, wine, whiskey, or other alcoholic beverages in the United States. Since many people still wanted to drink them, a huge "underground" business grew. This illegal business, much of it controlled by gangsters, was especially big in Chicago. Many shiploads of liquor were smuggled in from Canada through the Great Lakes. Gangsters like Al Capone and Bugs Moran are among the most well known characters in Chicago history. So many Hollywood movies have been made about them that, around the world, people immediately think *gangsters* when they hear the word *Chicago.*

After World War II, large num-

Al Capone *(left)* was one of Chicago's most well known gangsters.

bers of southern blacks came north to find work, greatly expanding the city's black population. Many Chicagoans moved out of older neighborhoods into new suburbs to the north, south, and west. Farmland and prairie suddenly turned into housing developments and shopping centers as Chicago's metropolitan area and population grew.

As the city has grown and changed, politics have played an important part in the day-to-day lives of Chicagoans. For the past fifty years, the city's politics have been controlled by one party, the Democrats. Chicago's most famous and longest-lasting Democratic mayor was Richard J. Daley. First elected in 1955, he served until his sudden death in

1976, when he was in his sixth term. Mayor Daley was known for his well-organized party "machine," which ran city services and rewarded loyal Daley supporters with appointed jobs.

Since Daley's time, some changes have come to the mayor's office. In 1979, Chicagoans elected Jane Byrne, the first woman to serve as mayor. Four years later, they elected Harold Washington, the city's first black mayor. The party "machine" is no longer as strong as it was when Daley ran city government.

Chicago history is full of stories—happy and tragic, noble and shameful. Many different individuals and groups have tried to find jobs, raise families, gain power, make money, and fight for justice and reform in an ever-changing city that is both tough and beautiful. Poet Carl Sandburg may have said it best when he called Chicago the "City of the Big Shoulders."

3

City of the World

Where could a person go who wanted to meet people from around the world, hear dozens of different languages and types of music, and eat food from many nations—without leaving the United States? That person could do all those things in Chicago, a city that has become home to people from almost everywhere.

Chicago has more Poles than any city but Warsaw. It has the largest Greek community in the United States, and is home to more Jews from Germany and Eastern Europe than any place but New York City or Israel. Chicago's 1,240,000 blacks, 256,000 Mexicans, 112,000 Puerto Ricans, 114,000 Germans, 105,000 Irish, and 86,000 Italians are all populations large enough to form cities in their ancestral homelands. There are also many thousands of Filipinos,

The people in this crowd reflect the ethnic heritage of many of Chicago's present-day citizens.

Swedes, Russians, Ukrainians, Chinese, Hungarians, Cubans, Koreans, Asian Indians, Japanese, Czechs, Slovaks, and Norwegians. The city has smaller numbers of people from many other ethnic groups.

Newer immigrants—such as Vietnamese, Mexicans, and Asian Indians—are more likely to live in ethnic communities and rely on their native languages more than English. Older groups—such as the Irish and Germans, who were among Chicago's earliest citizens—include some people who have little connection to their heritage. One Irish American may wear green on Saint Patrick's Day but give little thought to being Irish the rest of the year. Another may belong to Irish organizations, study Gaelic

(the Irish language), listen to Irish music, and vote for Irish politicians.

Many ethnic groups want to keep their languages and cultures alive, and make sure that new generations learn about them. On Saturday or Sunday, or after school, thousands of Chicago children go to special classes. They may attend Polish Saturday School, or Hebrew School, or study Croatian folk dances, or learn about Japanese traditions. They may attend kindergartens where they learn German, Italian, French, Greek, or Korean as well as English. On the weekends, families may attend parties or get together with groups of friends where everyone speaks Armenian or Spanish or Hindi. Even though these same people usually speak English at work or

A Chicagoan holds up a fish he caught from a pier along the lakefront.

Young Serbian Americans perform a traditional dance at the Serbian Cultural Club.

school, and live much like other Americans, it is important to them to keep the language and customs of their ancestors, too.

In the past, most Chicagoans lived in neighborhoods where their neighbors had the same ethnic background. There were Irish neighborhoods and Italian neighborhoods. Milwaukee Avenue, a famous road that runs through the city's North Side, was once known as "Polish Main Street." Lincoln Avenue was lined with German shops and businesses.

Illinois Governor James Thompson at an Asian American New Year's celebration.

Today, there are still neighborhoods that are identified with one ethnic group. Greektown has many Greek restaurants, Greek churches, and homes of Greek-speaking families. In Chinatown, there are Chinese restaurants, grocery stores, and other businesses run by several generations of Chinese Americans. Many families of Irish and Italian descent live in Austin, a neighborhood on Chicago's far West Side. Andersonville has Swedish shops, bakeries, and places to eat. In Germantown, U.S.A., it's

easy to find a sausage shop, import store, or bar where almost everyone speaks German. Many blacks live on the South Side and the West Side of the city. In some areas, most residents speak Spanish rather than English.

Today, though, it would be much more difficult to draw a map of Chicago's ethnic neighborhoods than it would have been a few generations ago. Now people of many backgrounds live throughout the city. A store with Spanish signs may be next door to one with Polish signs. A Korean church may be across the street from a Swedish bakery.

For thousands of Chicagoans, being part of an ethnic group is an important part of their lives. Many city residents also enjoy learning a little about the people who live in Chicago by going to different festivals, trying different kinds of food, and exploring shops and neighborhoods. Chicago is one of the few places in North America where a person can visit a Japanese Buddhist festival, eat Guatemalan and Thai food, shop in a store that sells Indian clothes or Ukrainian pastry, listen to live African music, and see a Lithuanian opera. For anyone who has an adventurous spirit, Chicago is truly a city of the world.

A Ukrainian Catholic church in Chicago.

4

Living—Chicago Style

More than three million people live within the city limits of Chicago, and another three million live in the many suburbs on the north, south, and west sides. The city is made up of dozens of neighborhoods, each with its own history, character, and special features. Because Chicago has such a variety of neighborhoods and people, its citizens have different ways of life.

Chicagoans, for example, live in many kinds of homes. Hundreds of tall skyscrapers filled with expensive apartments rise along the downtown lakefront in areas such as the Gold Coast. Some of these buildings are so big that a whole precinct—a district of city government—may be in just one building! People who live here may have long elevator rides each day to and from their homes on the 33rd or 59th story. They may spend as

High-rise apartment buildings line lakefront areas such as the Gold Coast.

much for a parking space in their building's garage as other people spend on an apartment!

Other less fortunate Chicagoans—some only a few blocks away from the Gold Coast area—live in public housing projects. One of these is the Cabrini-Green Homes project, where about fourteen thousand poor people live in crowded, dangerous, high-rise apartment buildings. These buildings may have broken elevators, garbage in the halls, and writing on the walls. Other poor people live in smaller, older buildings with boarded-up windows and plumbing that doesn't work.

Near the Gold Coast, and not far from Cabrini-Green, Carl Sandburg Village is a much different high-rise apartment complex. Many of its 6,000 residents are well-to-do young people who work downtown. Just to the west of Carl Sandburg Village lies a neighborhood known as Old Town. Here Chicagoans have repaired and restored charming old homes and enjoy the area's nightclubs and fine restaurants. New Town, a North Side neighborhood, has also changed for the better in recent years. Once an area of older, rundown homes, it began to change when young professional people moved in during the 1960s. The new residents repaired some of the old homes, built new homes and opened shops, restaurants, and small theaters. It is now a thriving community.

Many Chicago neighborhoods are

"Chicago bungalow" style homes on the city's West Side.

neither very rich nor very poor, although they, too, may be quite different from one another. These areas may look different because they were built at different times—the 1890s, the 1920s, or the 1950s, for example. Some have many small apartment buildings that are close together, and others have small single-family homes. (One style is called the "Chicago bungalow" because there are so many of them.) Neighborhoods also differ if they are near Lake Michigan, near large factories, or near a park.

Some have different styles because of the heritage of the people who live there—or who lived there in the past.

In many city neighborhoods, people are within walking distance of shops, schools, churches, libraries, and restaurants. Some Chicagoans, especially those living in or near the Loop, can walk to work. However, most drive cars or take public transportation—buses, trains, subways, and the El—to get from place to place. At any time of day or night, cars speed along the streets and highways, and people use public transportation or walk through the city.

Wherever Chicagoans live or work, young people must go to school. The city's public school system is the third largest in the United

An outdoor café in front of a Chicago apartment building.

States—about six hundred schools serving more than a half million students. Minorities—children of black, Hispanic, and Asian origin—are actually the majority in Chicago. Many schools, especially on the South Side where most of the population is black, have only black students. In other neighborhoods, people from different ethnic groups attend the same school. One high school's students speak more than fifty native languages!

Not all city children attend public school. Chicago has a large Catholic population, and more than one hundred thousand pupils attend Roman Catholic schools. Some religious groups—Lutherans, Jews, and Greek Orthodox, for example—also have pa-rochial schools. Other private schools serve certain ethnic groups, provide special education, or prepare students for college.

Chicago has a number of private and public colleges. The University of Chicago and Roosevelt University are well-known private schools. The University of Illinois at Chicago, which has 25,000 students, is the largest public college. Loyola and DePaul are Catholic universities.

Religion is important in the lives of many Chicagoans. Some attend various kinds of Protestant churches. Roman Catholic and Eastern Orthodox churches have larger memberships in Chicago than in most other U.S. cities. Some of these churches are connected with different ethnic

groups. Religious services are held in a number of languages—Polish, Korean, Ukrainian, Spanish, Russian, Croatian, and Vietnamese. Many black Chicagoans attend services where the joyous sounds of gospel music ring out from churchgoers of all ages. The city also has various Jewish congregations, as well as Buddhist temples, Moslem mosques, and other places where people gather to practice their religion.

Although Chicagoans have different religions and ways of life, they do have some things in common. All of them live in a great city, with crowds and excitement, danger and opportunity. Everyone has to cope with summer heat waves, winter blizzards, Chicago politics, and problems of crime and pollution. And all Chicagoans can enjoy the enormous variety of a fast-paced city that has much to offer people at work, school, or play.

Russian Americans in Chicago worship in this Russian Orthodox church.

5

A City of Adventures

If someone feels bored in Chicago, it's probably because he or she is in a bad mood—it can't be because "there's nothing to do!" Chicago is full of interesting places to go and ways to have fun.

Anyone who likes to read can go to one of the branch libraries, which are located in all parts of the city. Sometimes these libraries have story hours, movies, and concerts and plays. Downtown, the library's Cultural Center is a giant palace with huge rooms, beautiful old-fashioned decorations, and many programs for both adults and children.

Chicago's museums are wonderful places to visit, especially on a cold, gray winter day. At the Field Museum of Natural History, young people can see giant dinosaur skeletons and lifelike stuffed animals from faraway

These Chicagoans enjoy smelt fishing at night in Lake Michigan.

places. There are real mummies from ancient Egypt at the Oriental Institute of the University of Chicago. In the world-famous Museum of Science and Industry, visitors can climb into a German submarine, go down into a coal mine, walk inside a giant model of a human heart, and find out how oil is refined or how a telephone works. At smaller, specialized museums, Chicagoans learn about Chicago history or the history of many ethnic groups—blacks, Jews, Mexicans, Ukrainians, Lithuanians, and Italians.

The great Art Institute of Chicago has wonderful paintings and sculptures, and a special Junior Museum with programs and exhibits for children. Visitors to the Art Institute also enjoy the Thorne Rooms—miniature rooms from many times and places which have tiny, perfect furniture, rugs, dishes, and other objects that look exactly like real ones.

Children who live in Lincoln Park have seals, gorillas, and giraffes for neighbors. In the zoo near Lake Michigan, young Chicagoans can observe wild animals and visit a small "farm" with cows, goats, lambs, and other farm animals. Often, a special house for baby animals is open to visitors, who sometimes have parties to honor the zoo's residents. At Christmastime, people even sing carols to the animals!

The John G. Shedd Aquarium is a good place for anyone who likes "something fishy," because it has the world's largest indoor collection of

A popular exhibit in the Museum of Science and Industry is the "Fairy Castle." Designed and lighted by Hollywood experts, this enchanting castle has priceless miniature furnishings.

A baby armadillo enjoys lunch in the zoo nursery at Lincoln Park's new Pritzker Children's Zoo.

fish and other sea creatures. Here, visitors can see beautiful tropical fish in bright colors and funny shapes, and get a close-up view of the scary teeth of a shark. They can watch a diver feed a great variety of fish and turtles in the giant tank at the center of the aquarium.

Not far away is the Adler Planetarium, which has a dark theater with a special ceiling that looks like the sky. Lights projected on the ceiling show how the stars and planets move, how the sky looks in Australia, how it looked a thousand years ago, and how it might look in the future. It's science that seems more like magic.

Chicago has a famous symphony orchestra, many smaller groups of musicians, opera and dance companies,

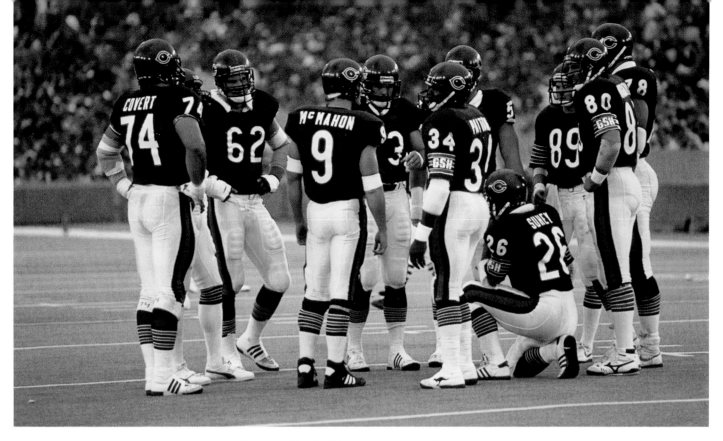

The Chicago Bears during a National Football League game at Soldier Field.

and dozens of theaters. Though most of their performances are for adults, some are especially for children.

Many Chicagoans are sports fans. All through the year, they have teams to cheer for. Fans can watch the Bulls play basketball, the Blackhawks play hockey, and the Sting play soccer. During the fall and winter, Chicago's football fans bundle up against the cold lake wind and head for Soldier Field to watch the Bears in action. With warmer weather in the spring comes baseball season. Then the city's baseball fans go to Comiskey Park on the South Side to cheer for the White Sox, or take the El to the North Side to Wrigley Field, home of the Cubs.

When the weather gets warm, Chicagoans flock to the city's miles of lakeside beaches and parks for sunbathing, picnicking, and swimming. There are many organized outdoor parties and picnics, too. Some are for the whole city—the Fourth of July concert and fireworks in Grant Park, the annual jazz and blues festivals, and "Taste of Chicago." At this event, restaurants set up dozens of booths that offer everything from Mexican to Ethiopian food. Gyros, Chicago-style pizza, bratwurst, burritos, ribs, and more can be found at Taste of Chica-

go. Several stages also present live entertainment for those who want to take a break from food.

Chicago has more parades than most cities. Two well-known ones take place on Polish Constitution Day (May 3) and Columbus Day (October 12). The whole city celebrates on Saint Patrick's Day (March 17), when a long, green parade winds through downtown. In fact, most everything turns green on Saint Patrick's Day. People wear green clothes, eat green cookies, and drink green beer. They even dye the Chicago River green just for the occasion!

Other celebrations are smaller. During the summer, neighbors rope off part of a street to have their own "block party" with food, music, and

The Chicago Police Piping Band marches in the Saint Patrick's Day Parade.

find your dreams

games. People from one of Chicago's ethnic groups may hold a picnic in a park with music and food from their ancestral homeland.

Sometimes, just for fun, Chicagoans go for a drive, or a ride on the bus or El, to look at interesting places. One beautiful trip is down (or up) Lake Shore Drive, where the lake is on one side of the highway, and hundreds of towering skyscrapers are on the other. Sometimes people travel on the water, too, in boats that go to the Loop, where they walk on busy, shop-filled streets such as Michigan Avenue or State Street. One part of Michigan Avenue is called the Magnificent Mile because it is filled with so many beautiful, expensive buildings. Part of State Street is closed to

A young Chicagoan sees a Christmastime display in a downtown store window.

cars, so people can walk along the mall. It's especially pretty in December, when stores put up colorful Christmas decorations and fancy displays in their windows. From all over the Chicago area, families come downtown to see the displays in Marshall Field's and Carson, Pirie, Scott. Children especially like the special scenery and moving dolls that show holiday customs and stories such as "The Night Before Christmas."

All over the city, there are shops and restaurants to explore. Giant toy stores, tiny antique shops, big department stores, fancy clothing stores, discount stores, hardware stores, and places to buy unusual gifts or special foods are everywhere. Just about everything a person could possibly buy or eat is somewhere in Chicago.

Chicagoans, like people everywhere, enjoy spending time with families and friends, eating meals, or just relaxing. Still, anytime someone is in the mood for excitement, there are plenty of adventures to find. Chicago is an American city with people and places that open a window to the world.

Places to Visit in Chicago

Museums

Adler Planetarium
1300 S. Lake Shore Drive
(312) 322-0300

Art Institute of Chicago
Michigan and Adams
(312) 443-3600

Balzekas Museum of Lithuanian Culture
6500 S. Pulaski
(312) 582-6500

Chicago Academy of Sciences
2001 N. Clark
(312) 549-0606

Chicago Historical Society
Clark and North
(312) 642-4600

Chicago Public Library Cultural Center
Michigan and Randolph
(312) 346-3278
The City Child in Summer programs are held at the Cultural Center from June to August. Special events include movies, story hours, and concerts and plays.

Du Sable Museum of African American History
740 E. 56th Place
(312) 947-0600

Express-Ways Children's Museum
2045 N. Lincoln Park West
(312) 281-3222

Field Museum of Natural History
Roosevelt Road at South Lake Shore Drive
(312) 922-9410
(312) 322-8854, weekend events

Italian Cultural Center
1621 N. 39th Ave., Stone Park
(312) 345-3842

Jane Addams' Hull House
800 S. Halsted
(312) 413-5353

Latvian Folk Art Museum
4146 N. Elston
(312) 588-2085

Mexican Fine Arts Center Museum
1852 W. 19th Street at Harrison Park
(312) 738-1503

Museum of Broadcast Communications
River City, 800 S. Wells
(312) 987-1500

Museum of Science and Industry
57th Street and South Lake Shore Drive
(312) 684-1414
*Includes a coal mine, a WWII German subma-
rine, and the new Henry Crown Space Center.*

Peace Museum
430 W. Erie
(312) 440-1860

Polish Museum of America
984 N. Milwaukee
(312) 384-3352

Spertus Museum of Judaica
618 S. Michigan
(312) 922-9012

Terra Museum of American Art
666 N. Michigan
(312) 664-3939

Ukrainian National Museum
2453 W. Chicago
(312) 276-6565

Plants and Animals

Brookfield Zoo
First Avenue and 31st Street, Brookfield
(312) 485-0263

Garfield Park Conservatory
300 N. Central Park
(312) 533-1281

Lincoln Park Conservatory
Fullerton and Stockton
(312) 294-4770

Lincoln Park Zoo
2200 N. Cannon Drive
(312) 294-4660

John G. Shedd Aquarium
1200 South Lake Shore Drive
(312) 939-2438

On Top of Chicago

Sears Tower Sky Deck
103rd Floor, 233 S. Wacker Drive
(312) 875-9696

John Hancock Observatory
94th Floor, 875 N. Michigan
(312) 751-3681

Professional Sports

Chicago Blackhawks Hockey
Chicago Bulls Basketball
Chicago Stadium
1800 W. Madison
(312) 733-5300 (Blackhawks)
(312) 943-5800 (Bulls)

Chicago Sting Soccer
Rosemont Horizon
Lunt and Mannheim, Rosemont
(312) 693-7000

Chicago Bears Football
Soldier Field
McFetridge Drive and Lake Shore Drive
(312) 294-2200

Chicago Cubs Baseball
Wrigley Field
1060 W. Addison
(312) 281-5050

Chicago White Sox Baseball
Comiskey Park
Wells and 35th
(312) 559-1212

Other Interesting Places

Facets Multimedia
1517 W. Fullerton
(312) 281-9075
Unusual films, including an afternoon children's series.

Navy Pier
Lakefront at Grand
This long dock extends into the lake; international ships unload their cargo, and various festivals and exhibits take place here during the year.

Water Tower Pumping Station
Michigan and Pearson
(312) 467-7114
The only Loop structure to survive the Great Fire. "Here's Chicago" includes exhibits, a film, and a slide show about the city.

Parks

Grant Park
Along Lake Shore Drive between Randolph and Roosevelt
(312) 294-2200

In summer, giant Buckingham Fountain flows, the rose garden blooms, and free concerts are presented by the Grant Park Symphony Orchestra, among others. Other festivities involve fireworks on July 4, Taste of Chicago, the Chicago Blues Festival, and the Chicago Jazz Festival.

The Chicago Park District runs 576 parks in the city, which have indoor and outdoor facilities for baseball, basketball, bicycling, bowling, archery, swimming, running, cross-country skiing, ice skating, volleyball, horseback riding, and other sports, as well as free or low-cost classes in sports, crafts, and other recreational activities. For information, call (312) 294-2493.

Additional information can be obtained from these agencies:

Chicago Tourism Council
806 N. Michigan Avenue
Chicago, Illinois 60611
(312) 280-5740

Illinois Department of Commerce
and Community Affairs
Department of Tourism
State of Illinois Center
100 W. Randolph, Suite 3-400
Chicago, Illinois 60601
(312) 917-7179

Chicago: A Historical Time Line

1779   Jean Baptiste Pointe du Sable opens a trading post and becomes Chicago's first non-native settler

1803   Fort Dearborn is built

1812   Fort Dearborn is destroyed

1818   Illinois becomes a state

1833   Chicago is officially incorporated as a town of 350 people

1837   Chicago officially becomes a city with a population of 4,117

1830-50   Growth of trade, transportation, and business builds Chicago into the Midwest's biggest city

1850s   Chicago street level is raised in giant construction project

1871   On October 8-9, most of the city is destroyed by the Great Fire

1893   Chicago hosts a giant world's fair, the Columbian Exposition

1920-33   Prohibition leads to booming underground business in alcoholic drinks; such gangsters as Al Capone and Bugs Moran become world famous and give Chicago a "tough city" reputation

1933   Chicago celebrates its 100th birthday with a fair, "Century of Progress"

1955-1976   Reign of Chicago's longest-lasting and most powerful mayor, Richard J. Daley

1979   Jane Byrne is elected Chicago's first woman mayor

1983   Harold Washington is elected Chicago's first black mayor

1988   Washington dies in office; Eugene Sawyer becomes mayor; lights installed in Wrigley Field for night baseball

Index